CW01095653

Follow Me

A Dog's View of the Gospel Story

By
Richard Symonds
and Ann Spokes Symonds

Published by
Robert Boyd Publications
260 Colwell Drive
Witney, Oxfordshire OX28 5LW

ISBN: 978 1 899536 82 5

First published 2006

Printed and bound at The Alden Press
De Havilland Way, Witney
Oxfordshire OX29 0YG

Front cover picture:
Christ washing the feet of the Apostles
by Tintoretto, painted 1545-50
Reproduced by kind permission of The Prado, Madrid

Illustrations

In memory of
Richard Symonds
and the dogs he loved

Acknowledgements

We should like to thank Marie and Carlos Ruiz for their invaluable help.

Also, we are much indebted to Paul Rimmer, Penny Nairne and Valerie Barnish for kindly reading the text and for their helpful suggestions. We should also like to thank all those owners of the copyrights of the Old Master paintings who have given permission for their reproduction to illustrate this story.

In one instance we were unable to locate the copyright holder of the picture. We have also tried to find the author of the verse which we include in the book but here again we failed to discover who the writer was.

SOME PREVIOUS BOOKS BY RICHARD SYMONDS

The Making of Pakistan, (Faber)
The British and Their Successors, (U.K.: Faber, U.S.A.: Northwestern)
Oxford and Empire, (U.K.: Macmillan and Oxford University Press,
    U.S.A.: St. Martin's Press)
*Alternative Saints: The Post Reformation British People Commemorated by the
    Church of England,* (U.K.: Macmillan, U.S.A.: St Martin's Press)
Far Above Rubies - The Women Uncommemorated by the Church of England,
    (Gracewing, Fowler Wright)
Inside the Citadel, Men and the Emancipation of Women 1850-1920, (U.K.: Macmillan,
    U.S.A.: St. Martin's Press)
In the Margins of Independence: A Relief Worker in India and Pakistan 1942-49,
    (Oxford University Press)

SOME PREVIOUS BOOKS BY ANN SPOKES SYMONDS

Celebrating Age (Age Concern, England)
Storks, Black Bags and Gooseberry Bushes (Paul Watkins)
The Changing Faces (series), local history of Oxford (Robert Boyd)
Havens Across the Sea (Mulberry Press)

Introduction

This book is about Tobias and is written by him. He was the dog which belonged to two of Jesus's disciples and he was not much more than a puppy when Jesus said to them 'Follow me'. Tobias followed too. He was called Tobias after the young Tobias who took his dog with him when he went on his travels with the angel Raphael. This is described in the Bible's Apocrypha.

We first came across Tobias when we were on holiday in Italy and visited the Duomo in Desenzano on Lake Garda. This church is dedicated to St Mary Magdalen. Above the altar in a large chapel within the church is a picture of the Last Supper by Gianbattista Tiepolo. This was painted between 1738 and 1743. There in the righthand front corner is the dog watching Christ and his disciples at the table.

This set us wondering where else did the dog go? Was he present during other events which were written about in the Gospels? We looked at many pictures by Old Master painters of the Gospel stories and often found dogs portrayed in them. In others the dog was left out but we think that Tobias might have been there.

Just as the artists had not been present at the time of the Gospels and so imagined what Jesus and his disciples looked like, so the artists did not know what Tobias looked like. That is why different kinds of dog appear in the pictures.

Any profits from the sale of this book will be given to animal charities.

Sadly, Richard Symonds died before this book was published. It is therefore dedicated to him.

Ann Spokes Symonds

The Dog's Story

My name is Tobias, the same as that of the only person mentioned in the Bible who took a dog with him on his travels. My own travels with the disciples were to be even stranger than those of Tobias' dog.

I wasn't much more than a puppy in the fishermen's family when Jesus came. I was lying in the bows of the boat and heard him say to James and John 'Follow Me, and I will make you fishers of men'. He had kind, compelling eyes and as he looked at me I was sure he meant me to come too. James told

Tobias and the
Archangel Raphael
by Titian

Tobias's dog looks on

"The Calling of the Sons of Zebedee" by Marco Basaiti (Active 1496-1530)

Jesus calls to James and John: "Follow me".

me to go back to the house and learn from my mother how to be a guard dog; but when I whimpered John said 'let him come. We'll need someone to play with at the end of the day after all the preaching'.

I soon found out my duties, as we were joined along the road between the villages on the lake by many other followers of the Master (the name they gave to Jesus). In the afternoons, when everyone snoozed, I kept off the thieves who tried to steal the clothes which were laid aside in the heat. I also prevented the village dogs making off with the food. And at the end of the day, as John had said, it seemed to cheer the disciples to have me around after they had been making all the kinds of mistakes which people do in new situations.

I would sit with James and John when the Master preached. As I heard his message again and again it seemed that it was meant for dogs as well as people. We must do our duty in the position in which God has placed us; and we must love and be loyal to the humans whom we meet.

It did not seem that at the beginning the Master wanted to be a healer: his intention was only to spread the news of the Kingdom. But he could not ignore the pathetic appeals for help from the blind and the crippled and people who had had strokes or had lost their minds. For how could they listen to the message when they were in pain and misery? As his marvellous powers as a healer came to be seen, he was mobbed by sufferers of every kind when we moved round the Lake.

One day he was teaching inside a house which was so crowded that it was impossible to get in or out. I was sitting outside the door, as I usually did, when I noticed that a hole was appearing in the roof. Dogs are more sensitive than humans to the tremors which come before an earthquake, which I supposed this to be. I rushed in through the people's legs and tried to pull James out, barking desperately as the ceiling began to fall in. Then through a huge hole there was gradually lowered on a bed a paralysed man whom his friends had been unable to bring in through the crowd. The Master was so struck by their faith and persistence that he cried out to the man 'Take up your bed and walk!' which he did, to the amazement of everyone.

Though people were often attracted to us because of the healings, many too came to the preaching because they wanted to know what was God's purpose for their lives.

Others expected to hear about the Kingdom whose arrival might bring happiness and prosperity for themselves and their children. Perhaps most of all came for the stories. The Master was a spell-binding story teller. He would pause in the middle to make sure that he was being understood. Then there would be shouts of 'Go on! Go on!' and 'Tell us what happened next'.

The villages around Lake Galilee, some of which are even small towns, are close together. News would spread from one to the next about the preaching, and when we reached it the people would demand to have the stories which they had heard about.

A great favourite was that of the Good Samaritan, though I thought myself that the traveller was foolish to walk alone along the road from Jerusalem to Jericho which was so well known to be a haunt of bandits. If, like the Good Samaritan, he had taken with him a couple of those fierce Kurdish dogs, which the shepherds breed to keep off the wolves, he might not have been attacked. People enjoyed the story because it showed up the lack of charity of the priest and Levite who did not stop to help the wounded traveller. Many had themselves experienced the unkindness of such superior people. The sympathetic character of the Good Samaritan who bound up the traveller's wounds made them wonder why the Jews would have nothing to do with the Samaritans just because they worshipped in a different temple. Samaritans began to be encouraged to come to our meetings.

Another story which was often asked for was that of the Prodigal Son who demanded his inheritance and went off to a far country to waste his money in riotous living, so that he even had to exist on the food which he stole from the pigs. I thought he, too, should have taken with him on his travels, a sensible dog who at least could have caught him something for his supper. When the young man came home, dismal and apologetic, his father welcomed him with a banquet and told off his jealous brother. The people loved this lesson, that God would forgive them for their follies if they said they were sorry. Everyone is in need of forgiveness, including dogs, which you can see as they cringe when they are scolded.

The Good Samaritan
by David Teniers II
(1610-1690) after
Francesco Bassano

"The Return of
the Prodigal
Son" by Murillo
1617–1682

Then there was a shorter story which was as much enjoyed for its amusement as well as its message. It was about a bothering or so called "Importunate neighbour" who came in the night and banged on the door of the next house to wake up the householder and borrow some food. The householder kept shouting that he was in bed with his children and could not get up, but in the end he opened the door grumpily, just to stop the noise. People were not only amused but comforted by the teaching that God will listen to one's prayers if they are persistent and sincere. In one of the pictures you can see dogs whose barking might have helped to cause the door to be opened.

The jolliest picnic in my life was the feeding of the five thousand. The accounts of it only mention the loaves and fishes. Much more important for dogs was water. I sniffed around until I found a clear running stream at the back of the mountain and barked people towards it. You might think from what has been said that the miracle was that 5 loaves and 2 fishes fed so many people. In fact almost everyone had brought their own food in their bags and pockets. The miracle was that they did not slink off behind trees to eat by themselves or just with their families.

Instead they shared all they had generously with their neighbours, whoever they might be . . . often people they would normally never speak to, let alone eat with. Tidy shopkeepers sat down with tanners and dyers whose dirty clothes and stained limbs would usually fill them with disgust.

"The
Importunate
Neighbour" by
W. Holman Hunt
1827-1910

The Miracle of the Loaves and Fishes by Giovanni Battista Pittoni (1687-1767)

23

Smart lawyers would listen patiently to mumbling shepherds. Respectable housewives would laugh with dancing girls although they would look down their noses at them at home. 'Love your neighbour'; even 'love your enemies' were the words they had been hearing. The love even overflowed to include the despised race of Dogs which the scriptures described with such contempt. Everyone petted me and gave me titbits.

The Master taught that not only all living things but flowers and plants had the right to be respected and cherished. So he made the people sit down in groups on the short grass which could come to no harm. After we finished eating there was a great clearing up of the rubbish, instead of leaving it to blow around.

There were many more adventures. There is the story of the Gaderene swine but it is not always told as it really happened. It is said that a devil which had possessed the sick man went into the swine. Not so. They became frightened by the noise of all the people shouting and cheering at the miracle of the healing of the sick man. When they ran away I could have rounded them up by nudging them away from the cliff, but some stupid people chased them so they were even more frightened and galloped down over the precipice and fell into the sea. The swineherds made up the story that the pigs were possessed by devils. They felt guilty, knowing that they had neglected to look after them while they watched what was happening and needed an excuse to give to their employers.

Nobody seemed to mind when I joined the wedding party at Cana. James tied a festive ribbon round my neck. I sat quietly at his feet with the children and morsels were thrown to me. As the party became rowdy, I had the feeling that a number of the guests were so jolly that they were unable to tell one wine from another, but of course I don't know about these things.

There was another party which I remember because through it I came to know two people whom I was often to see later. This was given in honour of the Master by a man called Simon at his house. I was dozing on the floor close to the Master's feet when I felt something dripping on to me. I looked up and saw a fine lady emptying a large alabaster vase of perfume on the Master's feet and drying them with her long golden hair. There was a bellow of indignation from someone who I found out to be Judas Iscariot. He shouted that this was a very expensive perfume which could have been sold and the money given to the poor.

When the Master, instead of rebuking the lady, said that her sins were forgiven her, Judas walked angrily out of the house. Passing me, with my ears dripping with coloured scent, he said 'You are a mess. Come along with me'. So we went for a walk, the first of many, as he simmered down and I dried out. The lady was Mary Magdalene who joined us on our travels.

One of the moments of which I was proudest was when the Master took me with him as he went to the house of Jairus to see his little girl who was thought to have died of a fever. As he raised her and said 'She is not dead but sleeping', mine was the first face she saw and she hugged me.

The Healing of the Man Born Blind by El Greco (Dominco Theotocopuli) 1541-1614

Reproduced by kind permission of State Arts Collection, Dresden.

Detail from "Feast at Cana' by Paolo Veronese

In the beginning when we were on the road no-one was really in charge of the arrangements. Most of the people who came to the preaching would go home in the evening. Some of the disciples had savings from their earlier earnings which helped to pay for the food if we were not invited to stay in homes in the villages. There were gifts of money and food too from people who came to the meetings. Soon, Judas Iscariot came to be our purse-bearer. When Judas went to see the moneychangers or to accept gifts he would often take me with him. He was usually a silent man but would sometimes burst out furiously at the wrongs of the Jewish people and the failure of their leaders to put these right. He liked my company because he could talk without being interrupted and pour out his scorn without fear of it being repeated.

The few women who were with us worked hard. They got up early before the preaching to see to the daily needs. They were fond of me and combed my coat and took care that I had food and water. I was closest to Mary Magdalene. With her wide experience she got on well with the men. But she disaproved of them being careless and not looking ahead and often told them so. While Judas Iscariot looked after the money, she did the shopping. She took me with her when she went to the markets, partly for company and also for protection in strange villages. She had a little cart made which I would pull along to carry the vegetables which we bought.

After a time the Master sent out the disciples two by two into the villages to spread the message . . . I went with James and John. We never knew what to expect. Sometimes we were listened to with respect and kindness and invited to stay. At others we were driven out fiercely by people whose way of life was upset by the message. With some families having a dog in the team helped, and the children would insist that we stay with them so that they could play with me. Others thought that dogs were unclean and unwelcome. Sometimes, when we were thrown out I think I helped James and John to see the amusing side of our situation as we recovered our breath.

We were not on the road all the time. Quite often we went back to our homes, specially in winter. Their father Zebedee had been unhappy when James and John left the house and the fishing business to follow the Master. Now that everyone in

Capernaum had heard of the great multitudes who came to the preaching and all the wonders which were done, he was proud in his silent way that his sons were in the Masters' inner circle. Their mother was delighted to have them back. She said they must have starved on the road and fed them up — and me too.

While James and John dealt with a pile of nets which needed mending, the Master would come and repair the boats. He was a careful and skilful carpenter. As he worked, he would ask the fishermen to tell him about the ways of fish and of the lake. He was a good listener, always wanting to learn about men and women's daily lives and problems. He used this knowledge in his preaching and made people in all kinds of jobs feel close to him.

He seemed to have sympathy with all living things. When I heard him speak about the birds, particularly the ravens, and of the hard lives they led in finding food for their families and materials for their nests, I was a little ashamed that I enjoyed chasing them. Perhaps most of all the Master enjoyed being with children. I would often be playing with them when the Master took them on his knee and told them the stories and I was allowed to listen.

The Scriptures were read aloud on the Sabbath, for the Master said he had come to fulfil, not to destroy them. Though I sat at a discreet distance, with my keen ears I could hear the reading. There was not much in it of cheer to dogs. Our name was used to describe persecutors, false teachers and unholy people. In the Psalms there were references to dumb dogs and greedy dogs, and people howled and prowled like dogs. One of the few encouraging things I heard was that Gideon had chosen as his best troops men who lapped water like dogs rather than those who drank it with their hands. And we met a kind lady who reminded the Master that dogs were allowed to eat the crumbs which fell from the children's table.

I was in one of the boats when the great storm blew up. I was not really frightened because I had swum in the lake ever since the children used to throw sticks for me to fetch as a puppy. But several of the disciples who could not swim were in something of a panic. People said later that the Master had calmed the waves but perhaps the miracle was rather, that he knew how to calm men who had lost their nerve.

"Christ washing the feet of the Disciples" by Jacopo Tintoretto (1518-1594)

Reproduced by kind permission of the Earl of Pembroke.

There is another version on the opposite page.

Christ Washing the feet of the Apostles by Jacopo Tintoretto, painted 1545-50

The disciples on the whole got on well together, without the better educated ones expecting to be treated as Top Dogs. James and John were happy to be known as ordinary fishermen by profession. But their mother, who was ambitious for them, came one day to ask the Master that when the Kingdom was created they should be seated on thrones on each side of him. The other disciples grumbled at this and the Master explained that the kingdom would not be one in which people were separated by rank. To teach this lesson he insisted, before supper, that he himself washed the feet of every disciple. I was allowed to watch and they were rather ashamed.

One day we were excited to hear that we were all going up to Jerusalem at the Passover. This time Zebedee saw us off with his blessing. Hundreds of people were with us — not only fishermen and shepherds and farmers from the countryside, but all sorts of townsmen, smiths and potters and tanners and many kinds of traders. Some brought wives carrying babies. Everyone was thrilled by the Master's message that it was easier for the poor than the rich to enter into the Kingdom. 'The Master says we must love one another', they shouted. They walked along together with people they would never have spoken to earlier. And though they had not heard much good about dogs in the scriptures the new love seemed to overflow to include me as I trotted along beside them.

We went merrily up the road, singing to prevent feeling tired, until we came to the gate of the Holy City. Great crowds came out to meet us and a man brought a young donkey for the Master to ride. He was not used to crowds and noise and was frightened, kicking up his heels. The Master had a calming way with him; I went ahead through the crowd telling the donkey to watch out for the tip of my tail and follow it.

When the procession arrived at the Temple, I was allowed into the forecourt. I had a fine view of what happened when the Master told off the money changers for turning God's house into a den of thieves. I barked with excitement when he upset the tables and the doves flew off and the lambs escaped from being sacrificed and everyone scrabbled for the coins which were rolling on the ground. I made so much noise that James tied me to a post further along the road.

In the next days the crowds thronged round us, expecting a mysterious Kingdom to be declared. The angry Jewish authorities planned to bring the movement and the Master himself to an end. I kept out of the way though, but as can be seen in a picture, I was present at the door during the Last Supper. This was the last meal Jesus had with his disciples. As I was dozing Judas Iscariot tiptoed out. When I wagged my tail and jumped up to go with him, he kicked me aside, which he had never done before.

Then the terrible things happened. I did not see them because James handed me over to Mary Magdalene and told her not to let me out of the house where she was staying. Only after the Master's death was I allowed out into the sad room where the disciples spent their time in prayer.

Part of
The Last Supper
by Giavanni
Batista Tiepolo,
painted 1738-43.
In the Duomo,
Desenzano, Lake
Garda, Italy.

"Christ at Emmaus" by Paolo Veronese 1528-1588

Reproduced by kind permission of the Louvre, Paris.

One day two of the disciples felt that they needed to get out and take a walk. I was allowed to go with them to a village near Jerusalem called Emmaus. As they were walking along, talking about all the things that had happened to them, a stranger joined them. I knew at once that he was the Master, for dogs always recognize people by the scent. I wagged my tail but did not jump up for I had been taught to treat him with special respect. At first the disciples did not realize who he was. Only when we arrived at Emmaus did they recognise him (while two little girls made friends with me) when he blessed the bread and broke it, as was the Master's custom. Then we rushed back to Jerusalem and told the others the amazing news that we had met the Master.

I was with the disciples in Jerusalem when the Holy Spirit came down to inspire them to go out into all lands to spread the Master's message. I did not have a place in this. It was not because I would have been a nuisance in the travels. James and John were afraid of what would happen to me when they were likely to have stones thrown at them. Also they could be locked up in cells where I would not be allowed to be with them and might starve outside.

So they took me back to Capernaum when they went to say goodbye to their parents. And there I have guarded the house and looked after the goats and gone out with the fishermen. I always remember the great adventures with the Master and his kindness. Sometimes as I lie in the sun I feel that although I am an animal of no importance the Master's message was, and is, to me as well as to the people. And I wonder if it is only an accident that God spells Dog backwards.

The authors
with their dog
Dantë

Richard
with
Raffles

Recently we have come across this verse in two separate publications:

When God made the earth and sky
And all the flowers and trees
He then made all the animals
And all the birds and bees
And when his work was finished
Not one was quite the same
God said, `I'll walk this earth of mine
And give each one a name.'

And so he travelled land and sea
And everywhere he went
A little creature followed him
Until its strength was spent.
When all were named upon the earth
And the sky and sea
The creature said `Dear Lord
There's not one left for me'.

The Father smiled and softly said
`I've left you to the end.
`I've turned my own name back to front
And called you Dog, my friend'.

Anon